Sermons on the Savior

Sermons on the Savior

Douglas G. Denton

BAKER BOOK HOUSE
Grand Rapids, Michigan 49516

To the memory of my father,
who came to know
the Subject of these sermons personally

Copyright © 1990 by Baker Books
a division of Baker Book House Company
P.O. Box 6287, Grand Rapids, MI 49516-6287

ISBN: 0-8010-3000-5

Second printing, July 1994

Printed in the United States of America

Scripture quotations in this book are based on the King James
Version of the Bible.

Contents

Part 3
The Sayings of the Savior

Preface

Many times a pastor wishes to preach a short (seven-to-ten-week) series of sermons around a certain theme. No greater subject can be found than that of our Lord himself: his birth, works, words, death, and resurrection.

These messages are arranged according to various aspects of Jesus' life and ministry. Some are seasonal; others would be appropriate anytime. All are expository rather than topical.

May these outlines provide a framework for the preacher's own creativity as he endeavors to expound the Word of God with faithfulness and to exalt the Savior with power.

Douglas G. Denton

Part 1

The Birth of the Savior

1

The Prince with Four Titles

Scripture Reading: Isaiah 9:6, 7

The world is enamored of the British royal family. The media follows the personal lives of Prince Charles and Diana and Prince Andrew and Sarah with a zeal that borders on harassment. Although they refer to them as "Chuck and Di" and "Andy and Fergie," their formal titles are much more impressive and numerous.

But all titles pale in comparison with those of the Lord Jesus Christ. The prophet Isaiah gives us four of his more significant ascriptions.

I. **Wonderful Counselor**
   A. The birth, life, miracles, teachings, death, and resurrection of Christ produced wonder and amazement on the part of all those who witnessed or heard about them (Luke 2:18; 24:4; Matt. 7:28; 27:14, and so forth).
   B. Those who follow the counsel of Jesus' teachings and example will have unsurpassed wisdom. John calls him "the Word" (1:1), a term sometimes used synonymously with reason and judgment. (*See also* Proverbs 8:14; James 1:5.)

II. **Mighty God**
   A. The power of Christ was evident in his miracles. He demonstrated his might over demons, disease, nature, enemies, and even death.

B. The deity of Christ is the bedrock of the Christian faith. The New Testament writers affirm it unequivocally.

III. Everlasting Father
A. The divinity of Christ implies his eternal existence. But we need not infer it, for this truth is clearly stated (John 1:1).
B. There is no confusion of the persons of the Trinity here. Christ is Father in the sense that he was the agent of creation and the author of eternal life.

IV. Prince of Peace
A. A prince is not just the son of a king; he is a ruler. Our Lord has the same authority as God the Father, and he will reign over the kingdom of God.
B. The angels proclaimed "peace on earth" at Jesus' birth (Luke 2:14), and he pronounced a blessing on the peacemakers (Matt. 5:9). The apostle Paul said of him, "He is our peace" (Eph. 2:14).

These are only a fraction of the titles of Christ, but they help reveal the many-faceted character of the Savior.

2

The Miraculous Birth of Christ

One cannot read the Gospel narratives of the nativity without being struck by the abundance of supernatural elements: choirs of angelic beings, strange astronomical phenomena, visits from foreign astrologers, prophetic predictions in the temple precincts. Remove these strands from the Christmas story and the fabric of the incarnation unravels into nothing.

Yet if we accept the miraculous as the very warp and woof of the nativity, there is much we can learn. The birth of the Savior

I. **Is Miraculous in His Conception (vv. 18, 20)**
   A. We are explicitly told that at the time Mary was discovered to be with child, she and Joseph had not yet come together, being only espoused (betrothed, not married). Her virginity is clearly asserted.
   B. Twice Matthew says that Mary's pregnancy is "of" the Holy Spirit. By some supernatural operation of God's Spirit, the womb of a virgin was made fertile without the agency of a human male.

II. **Is Miraculous in His Commission (vv. 21, 25)**
   A. The very name *Jesus* implies his mission, for it means "Jehovah is salvation." Jesus became incarnate to accomplish our deliverance from sin and Satan.
   B. He is also clearly said to be the Savior, not just as a hope or a goal or a prediction, but as a future cer-

tainty: "He *shall* save his people from their sins" (italics added).

III. Is Miraculous in His Condescension (vv. 22, 23)
    A. Isaiah 7:14 and 9:6 prophesied that God would send a Savior, even stating the fact of his virgin birth. Matthew notes the fulfillment of these predictions.

    B. As Immanuel (God *with* us), Jesus condescended to become one *of* us; not a demigod (half-man, half-god) but as the God-Man.

Let us never think that we shall make the Christian faith more palatable today by jettisoning the miraculous. Such "demythologizing" only robs us of the wonder of Christmas.

3

Three Reactions to the Incarnation

Have you ever spoken to people on the street only to have them snub you? Suppose they actually assaulted you in return for your friendliness.

When God became a man, he spoke to the world in love. That greeting met with three responses at the first Christmas. Little has changed.

I. **The Reaction of Adoration (vv. 1, 2, 10, 11)**
   A. The Magi made the long journey from Persia to worship the Christ child. They acknowledged him as Son of God and King of Kings.
   B. When the star had led them to him, they presented him with gifts, tokens of their homage and adoration. These gifts were both expensive and symbolic.
   C. Millions today still respond to the birth of Christ by offering him worship and sacrifices. Is this your reaction too?

II. **The Reaction of Indignation (vv. 3, 13, 16–18)**
   A. King Herod "the Great," executioner of all who threatened his throne (including members of his own family), was outraged at the news of the birth of a potential rival and vowed to destroy him.
   B. Fear turns to indignation and anger when we seek

to be our own absolute authority, yielding control of our lives to no one, not even God.

C. How many today refuse to descend the throne of their lives and abdicate to the rightful King? They also see the birth of Christ as the threat of a rival, not as the arrival of a Savior.

III. The Reaction of Preoccupation (vv. 5, 6)

A. How ironic that the religious leaders were too busy with their priestly duties to attend the greatest religious event in history! A distance of five miles was too great for them to travel.

B. Perhaps this reaction is the most tragic of all. Casual indifference to Jesus' birth lacks even the zeal of Herod's hatred.

C. This is probably the most common reaction of modern people. We are too preoccupied with our Christmas shopping and office parties to acknowledge the real meaning of Christmas.

What is your reaction to the birth of the Savior? Anything less than adoring worship is an insult to God's most gracious greeting in the person of his Son.

4

The Worship of the Wise

Scripture Reading: Matthew 2:1–11

So many myths have grown up about the Magi that we confuse historical fact with literary legend. It is folklore, not Scripture, that says there were three of them, they rode camels, and they were kings.

Matthew simply calls them "wise men" who came to worship the newborn King. Wise men still worship him, and that worship

I. Propels a Great Pilgrimage (vv. 1, 2)
   A. The Magi undertook a long and arduous journey to find the Christ child. Theirs was a physical pilgrimage of many miles.
   B. Many a wise man has embarked on an intellectual quest—a spiritual journey toward God—and have likewise found him in the manger of Bethlehem.

II. Produces Great Rejoicing (v. 10)
   A. When the Magi saw his star, they rejoiced because they knew their search was nearing its end. The fulfillment of their quest was about to be realized.
   B. Finding Christ always results in joy. Those who look for happiness will never find it until they seek instead for Jesus.

III. Prompts a Great Sacrifice (v. 11)
   A. The gifts of the Magi were both costly and appropriate. They had intrinsic value as well as symbolic worth.

B. True worship inevitably moves us to offer our best
    to our Lord. It prompts us to give our lives to him
    as a living sacrifice (Rom. 12:1, 2).

The worship of the wise is the adoration of those who have
sought for and found God in Christ. They have discovered the
joy that worship brings. No gift is too dear to lay before him, not
even the gift of ourselves.

5

Getting Ready for Christmas

Scripture Reading: Luke 1:26–38

Are you ready for Christmas? Have you finished your holiday preparations: shopping, baking, cleaning, mailing cards, and wrapping gifts?

What about your spiritual preparations? Here are some steps to take to get ready to celebrate the birth of Christ in a way that will make this a most memorable Christmas.

I. Receive Its Message with an Open Mind (v. 29)
   A. Mary's reaction to the angelic announcement was a model of openness. She neither flippantly accepted the startling message nor skeptically dismissed it.
   B. All that God requires of us in the beginning is that we not *dis*believe the message of Christmas. Not to keep an open mind about the incarnation is not only sinful and dangerous, it is unreasonable. Give the gospel a fair hearing.

II. Reflect Upon Its Meaning with an Inquiring Heart (v. 34)
   A. Mary, quite naturally, had some questions. She desired a deeper understanding of this unique event. Perhaps she was chosen because of her contemplative nature (Luke 2:19, 51).
   B. We will be better prepared to make the most of Christmas if we will take time out from our busy physical preparations to ponder the spiritual significance of this holy day.

III. **Respond to Its Mission with an Obedient Will (v. 38)**
   A. The annunciation required Mary's permission and participation. Her cooperation was necessary if she were to carry and deliver God's Messiah. She willingly accepted this mission.
   B. Christmas calls each of us to a task. We who celebrate the birth of Christ have a mission to call others to join us in worshiping the incarnate Son of God.

Are you ready for Christmas? Are your spiritual preparations complete? Are your heart and mind poised in anticipation? If so, you may be in for the greatest Christmas season of your life!

6

"He Shall Be Called . . ."

Scripture Reading: Luke 1:31–35

In ancient times names were carefully chosen to express the character, position, or hope of the person they described. Thus when the angel Gabriel announced that a name had already been selected for one yet unborn, that name must have great significance.

In this passage, the angel mentions three names or titles of the Holy Child. He says that he shall be called

I. **"Jesus," for He Is the Savior (v. 31)**
   A. Our Lord has perhaps three hundred titles in Scripture but only one personal name. Among his titles are: Christ (Messiah), Immanuel (God with us), Son of Man, Prince of Peace, Son of David, Son of God.
   B. But his name is "Jesus," meaning "Jehovah is salvation"—a most appropriate name for the Savior who delivered us from sin, death, and hell.

II. **"The Son of the Highest," for He Is the King (vv. 32, 33)**
   A. This title speaks of our Lord in his royal and majestic character. Jesus is the heir apparent to the throne of David.
   B. But more than that, he is heir to the throne of God. He is king, not of the Jews only, but over all humankind: "He shall reign . . . for ever; and of his kingdom there shall be no end."

III. **"The Son of God," for He Is the Lord (v. 35)**
  A. If the Gospels (indeed the New Testament) teach anything, it is the deity of Christ. He is not, like the demigods of pagan mythology, half-man and half-god. Rather, he is *Immanuel, God with us, very God of very God.*
  B. Yet he is as completely human as he is completely divine. This is an unfathomable mystery, but it is nonetheless true.

Jesus is the Savior, the King, the Son of God. But is he *your* Savior, King, and Lord? Making him so is what Christmas is all about.

7

Simple Steps to a Merry Christmas

Scripture Reading: Luke 2:8–20

It seems that every Christmas there is at least one present that has to be put together before it can be used: a bicycle, a model airplane, a doll house. Fortunately these usually come with instructions, which we read when all else fails!

Christmas itself comes to us, in a sense, unassembled in that there are steps we must take to make it merry. It is a good thing for us that Christmas, too, comes with a book of instructions! Here are the steps the Bible recommends for making Christmas merry.

I. **Step One: Seek and Find (vv. 15, 16)**
   A. The shepherds, following the angelic announcement, decided to "go and see" the blessed event for themselves. They "came and found" the Babe lying in a manger, a most unlikely place for a merry Christmas!
   B. A joyous yuletide is not to be found at the shopping mall, the office party, or under the tree. It is found at a cattle trough in a lowly stable in Bethlehem.

II. **Step Two: Go and Tell (v. 17)**
   A. The shepherds increased their merriment by spreading the good news of Jesus' birth.
   B. Trying to keep Christmas to ourselves is to rob not only others but ourselves of its true joy. By wit-

24

nessing to it we take an important step toward a
merry Christmas.

III. Step Three: Hear and Wonder (v. 18)

    A. The very familiarity of the Christmas story may, if
we are not careful, cause it to lose its wonder for
us. Those who first heard it from the lips of the
shepherds were struck by the wonder of it, awed by
the mysterious and miraculous nature of their tale.

    B. If we can succeed in recapturing the wonder of the
story, we shall have taken a giant step toward a
bright holiday season.

IV. Step Four: Keep and Ponder (v. 19)

    A. Mary "kept" or remembered everything that hap-
pened in connection with the birth of her child. She
meditated on the meaning of those things.

    B. To keep is also to *observe,* to *celebrate.* As we
observe the Christmas season and celebrate the
birth of Christ, let us contemplate its deepest significance. Our Christmas will be the merrier for it.

V. Step Five: Return and Praise (v. 20)

    A. "The shepherds returned" to their flocks and
responsibilities, but they did so "glorifying and

praising God." They went back to the same jobs, but they were not the same men. The merriment of Christmas had changed them into people of praise.

B. Have you allowed Christmas to make a positive difference in your life? Do you return to work after the holidays, praising God for the gift of his Son and rejoicing in a merry Christmas?

These five steps are simple, but that does not mean they are easy. It took some effort on the part of the shepherds and of Mary to get the most out of Christmas. If your holidays have not been merry in the past, this year try reading and following the instructions!

Part 2

The Introduction
of the Savior

8

The Coming of the King

Jesus Christ is not only the King of the Jews, he is King of kings and Lord of lords. It is said in God's Word that he will rule the nations with a rod of iron (Rev. 2:27) and that at the name of Jesus every knee shall bow (Phil. 2:10). His entrance onto the stage of history was truly the coming of the King.

I. The King's Coming Was Preceded by a Messenger (vv. 1–4, 6)

    A. In ancient times when a king was to pay a royal visit to some part of his realm, it was customary to send a herald ahead of him to alert the people. This gave them an opportunity to prepare for the regal visit by repairing roads, whitewashing buildings, disposing of rubbish.

    B. John the Baptist was Christ's herald who bade the people prepare for his coming by repenting of their sins and clearing the way for his entrance into their lives.

    C. As the King came into this world, so he wants to come into our hearts. We have been warned of his coming and of his coming again. Let us prepare ourselves to receive him.

II. The King's Coming Was Heeded by the Multitudes (v. 5)

    A. John's message of warning "got through" to large numbers of people. They flocked out of the city and into the wilderness to listen to John's announcement of the coming of the King.

B. John urged them to do three things to get ready for the arrival of the Messiah: *repent* of their sins; *bear fruit* as evidence of their repentance; and *be baptized* as a symbol of their need for spiritual cleansing.

C. John's baptism was the baptism of repentance; it was not Christian baptism. It did not commemorate our identification with Christ in his death, burial, and resurrection.

III. The King's Coming Was Needed by All Humankind (vv. 7, 8)

A. No one was more aware than John that water baptism could not wash away a person's sins. What was called for was a baptism of fire, the inward cleansing of the soul by the Holy Spirit.

B. Only Christ could bring that real baptism of which water baptism was but a picture. By his death on the cross Jesus met the need of all humankind for salvation and forgiveness.

C. The need for the coming of the King to save us from our sins has not changed in two thousand years. Have you allowed the King to meet your need of salvation?

The coming of the King was the greatest visitation the world has ever known or ever will know until that same King comes again. Despite John's warning, many were unprepared the first time he came. May we not make the same mistake.

9

The Commissioning of the King

Scripture Reading: Mark 1:9–11

The inauguration of a newly elected president of the United States, gala affair that it is, is a simple ceremony compared to the coronation of a British monarch. Queen Elizabeth II was crowned on June 2, 1953, in Westminster Abbey, amid such pageantry that those who witnessed it say they will never forget.

Yet when the King of kings began his public ministry there was no coronation nor even an inauguration—but there was a kind of installation or commissioning service. The baptism of Jesus, rustic as it was, may be seen as the commissioning of the King.

I. **It Was Symbolized by the Water (v. 9)**
   A. Among the first meanings of water baptism is identification. Before Jesus could lead the movement to bring in the kingdom of God, he had to join it, to become identified with it and its adherents.
   B. John the Baptist, by baptizing Jesus, was symbolically commissioning him for messianic service.

II. **It Was Visualized by the Dove (v. 10)**
   A. A king must also be anointed. In Bible times it was customary to anoint a king with oil, as was done with Saul, David, and Solomon.
   B. This ceremony depicted the anointing of the Holy Spirit. When Jesus was baptized, the Holy Spirit descended in bodily form like a dove. This was

visual proof that the person and work of Christ had
the unction of God's Spirit.

III. It Was Verbalized by the Voice (v. 11)
   A. The Jews spoke of the *bath qol*, the "daughter of
   sound." Because God dwelt in the remote regions
   of the highest heaven, it was thought that men
   could only hear the faraway echo of his voice.
   B. Here the very heaven opened and God spoke
   directly, clearly, and audibly. The Father verbally
   gave his approval to the commissioning of his Son
   as Messiah and King.

It is appropriate that Jesus was commissioned rather than
crowned at the inception of his public ministry, for he came on a
mission of peace and an errand of mercy. Though he is King, he
came as a servant of God to seek and to save those who are lost.

10

The Temptation of the King

Scripture Reading: Mark 1:12, 13

In December of 1776 Thomas Paine penned these famous words: "These are the times that try men's souls." It is the universal lot of all men to endure times of testing.

Since our Lord is Son of man as well as Son of God, he, too, had to face temptation. Like ours, his time of trial

I. Was a Consequence of Commitment

A. Jesus' wilderness testing followed "immediately" upon the heels of his baptism. No sooner had he dedicated his life to doing God's will in his unique role than he was severely tested.

B. Do not be surprised if you find that soon after you dedicate (or rededicate) your life to Christ, you are tempted by the devil.

II. Was Inherent in Providence

A. It was the impulse of God's Spirit that drove Jesus into his temptation ordeal, even though God himself tempts no one (James 1:13). God allows Satan to tempt us to make us stronger.

B. We can resist temptation, just as Christ did, for the same resources that he employed against Satan are available to us: the Word of God and the Holy Spirit.

III. Was One Instance of Experience
   A. Our Lord's triumph over Satan in the wilderness was only the victory of a single battle. He was to face his ancient foe in many future combats, culminating in the cross. It took many conquests before Satan was finally vanquished at Calvary.
   B. We must not think that because we win one battle we have defeated the tempter for all time. If we do, we become vulnerable to his subsequent attacks.

Our Savior knows the power of temptation and our human frailty because he himself went through testing. Because he experienced trial, he can not only sympathize but aid us in obtaining victory (Heb. 4:15).

11

The Kingdom of the King

Scripture Reading: Mark 1:14, 15

Most of us have heard a good many sermons (if not many good ones). But what must it have been like to hear Jesus preach? For Mark says that "Jesus came . . . preaching."

What was the subject of our Lord's sermons? According to this passage, it was the welcome announcement that the long-awaited reign of the Messiah was about to commence. Jesus said

I. **The Kingdom Is Temporally Near (vv. 14, 15a)**
   A. *Time* here means a seasonable or opportune time. It stresses the *quality* rather than the *quantity* of time. That is, the time is ripe—all conditions are favorable for the coming of God's kingdom.
   B. There comes to us a rare window of opportunity when circumstances are auspicious for our acceptance of the gospel. God help us if we let that time slip away without becoming a part of God's kingdom.

II. **The Kingdom Is Spatially Near (v. 15b)**
   A. The phrase "is at hand" is literally "has drawn near." The kingdom has arrived in the person of the King. It is as close as the presence of Jesus.
   B. The kingdom of God is not something light years from us in a galaxy far, far away. It is not bound by geography to Jerusalem or even to a distant "heaven." If Christ is in our hearts, then "the kingdom of God is within you" (Luke 17:21).

III. The Kingdom Is Personally Near (v. 15c)

    A. The keys to the kingdom are repentance and faith. Those who believe in Christ do not have to wait until some distant future to enter the kingdom or for the kingdom to enter them.

    B. There is still an urgency about Jesus' command to repent and believe, for time is rapidly running out. Only we can make the kingdom personal by our acceptance of the King.

The kingdom has drawn near to you, but have you drawn near to it? Jesus once told a scribe, "You are not far from the kingdom of God" (Mark 12:34). But "not far" is not *close*, much less *in*. How near are you to merging with God's kingdom?

12

The Call of the King

Scripture Reading: Mark 1:16–20

In Jack London's famous story "The Call of the Wild" a sled dog is torn between loyalty to his human masters and the call of the Alaskan wilderness in his blood.

There is a call that is heard by people, a call extended by the King nearly two thousand years ago. They are still hearing and answering his call.

I. The King Enlists Common Men (vv. 16, 19)

    A. These first disciples recruited by our Lord were not remarkable for their education, accomplishments, influence, nor piety. They were simple "blue-collar" laborers, practical fishermen.

    B. Had Jesus been looking for mystics, he would likely have gone to India; for philosophers, to Athens; for rabbis, to Jerusalem. Instead he went to the shores of a small lake and enlisted some ordinary men whom he could use in extraordinary ways.

II. The King Extends a Compelling Call (vv. 17, 18, 20)

    A. We are struck by the apparent lack of hesitation on the part of these levelheaded businessmen. Even more rare is the instant agreement on the part of two sets of business partners! So compelling was the King's call for them to follow him.

    B. Have you heard the compelling call of Christ to follow him? He still calls today through the preaching

"

of the gospel and the drawing power of the Holy Spirit.

III. The King Evokes a Complete Response (vv. 18, 20)
   A. To abandon a few fishing nets is a small thing, but these men turned their backs on their homes, jobs, possessions, and families. They forsook everything in total commitment to Christ.
   B. The King beckons us to leave behind everything that would hinder our walk with him. Nothing less than absolute dedication to his will can truly be called discipleship.

None of us is so ordinary that Christ will not call us. None should be so obstinate as to resist that call. And none can follow him who will not abandon everything for the privilege of being his disciple.

13

The Authority of the King

Scripture Reading: Mark 1:21–28

Authority is one of those "hot" words today. Ever since the 1960s it has been fashionable to question authority, whether that of government over its citizens, teachers over their students, or parents over their children.

This is not as new as it may seem, for authority has always been controversial. Certainly it was so when Jesus came teaching "as one who had authority." The authority of the King

I. Was Implied by His Teaching Method (vv. 21, 22)
    A. It had long been the custom for rabbis, in their teaching, to quote extensively the opinions of earlier rabbis. In true legalistic fashion they depended heavily upon precedents, and the emphasis was on laws and rules and interpretations of these.

    B. Jesus appealed to no human teacher or tradition but spoke as one who had God's endorsement to make his own pronouncements. He cited no "expert opinions," for he was the greatest authority on God's Word and will.

II. Was Defied by an Unclean Spirit (vv. 23, 24)
    A. The foul entity that possessed the soul of its poor, unfortunate victim challenged Jesus' right to interfere in its malignant business. It attempted to gain power over Christ by the old magic trick of naming one's enemy.

    B. Defiance of Jesus' authority, even by a supernatural

being, is futile. It could no more resist the authority
of the King than we can.

III. Was Verified by His Miraculous Power (vv. 25, 26)
   A. In contrast to the self-styled exorcists of the day,
   Jesus used no magic spells, no incantations, no ritual ceremonies. He simply commanded and the
   demon obeyed.
   B. If there was any doubt among the crowd about the
   authority that Jesus claimed, it was dispelled by
   this miracle. He had gone beyond assuming authority to demonstrating it.

IV. Was Confirmed by the Astonished Reaction (v. 27)
   A. The word here translated "amazed" carries not only
   the idea of shock but also the notion of terror. The
   people were thunderstruck, paralyzed with fear.
   B. People still find Jesus' authority very disconcerting
   when they first discover that he is not just another
   religious teacher but the Son of God who claims the
   right of lordship over every life.

V. Was Magnified by His Spreading Fame (v. 28)
   A. As more and more folks heard about Jesus, they
   sought him out. Many of these went on to become
   his disciples.
   B. Jesus' fame is still spreading. It is our task, as his
   followers, to make his name known everywhere
   and to persuade people to acknowledge his rightful
   authority.

Of all people, Christians ought to be the first to submit to
Jesus' authority. Yet thousands who profess Christ do not witness
or tithe or do anything else he has commanded us to do.

14

The Providence of the King

Scripture Reading: Mark 1:29–31

Every father of a daughter hopes that when his little girl grows up she will marry a good provider. He desires that his son-in-law will be the kind of husband who will meet the spiritual and emotional needs of his family as well as their material needs.

Jesus Christ, as the heavenly Bridegroom, is the perfect provider for his bride, the church. He exercises providential care over her in love. In this passage we see an example of the providence of the King.

I. The Opportunity for It—Fellowship (v. 29)
   A. Jesus and his disciples had just come from the synagogue service. Having fellowshiped with God, they were on their way home to fellowship with one another around the dinner table.
   B. If you do not seem to experience divine watchcare in your life, you might want to check on your fellowship with God and with other Christians through church attendance and activities.

II. The Occasion of It—Infirmity (v. 30a)
   A. The specific situation that led to Jesus' intervening help was a physical illness on the part of Simon's mother-in-law. Our Lord saw her need as an opportunity to minister God's loving care.
   B. There are all kinds of infirmities other than physical illness. People have mental, financial, and spiritual problems that Christ can meet in a providential

way. Perhaps he wants to use us as his instruments
of ministry.

III. The Origin of It—Prayer (v. 30b)
   A. Strictly speaking, God's providence originates in
      his character. But it begins to benefit us only when
      we turn to him for help.
   B. As soon as it was discovered that Simon's wife's
      mother was ailing, they took their need to Jesus and
      asked for his assistance. Prayer was the catalyst in
      her healing.

IV. The Object of It—Wholeness (v. 31a)
   A. Here we see the healing touch of the Master's hand.
      Gently he raised the feverish woman from her
      couch and restored her to health and wholeness.
   B. Not everyone who is physically sick will be healed,
      but all of us can know spiritual healing as our sin-
      sick souls are made whole and well. This is the
      object of God's providence.

V. The Outcome of It—Ministry (v. 31b)
   A. That Simon's mother-in-law immediately began to
      wait on her guests says a great deal about her. She
      was "saved to serve."
   B. It is Christ's intention that our healing result in ser-
      vice to others. It is not an end in itself; the ultimate
      goal of wholeness is that we become ministers to
      others of God's grace.

How comforting it is to know that the providence of God, his
protecting watchcare over us, is part of the character of Jesus. He
is ever present with us in fellowship and spiritual healing. Let us
use our wholeness in service to others in need.

15

The Celebrity of the King

An early television program called "What's My Line?" featured a distinguished panel that tried to guess contestants' occupations. The high point of the show was the appearance of a "mystery guest," a celebrity whose identity the panel was to discover by asking only *yes* and *no* questions.

When Christ the King came among men, he soon became well known. He gained an almost instant popularity and became something of an overnight celebrity. As such, people were curious about his identity.

I. His Personality Appealed to the People (vv. 32, 33)

A. As soon as the Sabbath was ended "at even," crowds flocked to him. There was something magnetic about his compassion, his wisdom, even his humor.

B. He is the most attractive, appealing, winsome person who ever lived. People are still drawn to this charismatic, confident, and caring Savior.

II. His Authority Healed the People (v. 34a)

A. News of his miracles of the previous day spread like wildfire. He had commanded both disease and unclean spirits to depart the minds and bodies of their victims, and it was so.

B. Never had anyone exercised such authority over malignant forces, both personal and impersonal. Jesus heals the whole person.

III. His Identity Was Concealed from the People (v. 34b)
   A. No doubt, one reason why Christ did not allow the devils to reveal who he was had to do with who they were. But also he knew that a premature knowledge of his identity by the Jewish leaders would mean they would seek his life before he had a chance to complete his earthly ministry.
   B. Now, however, we are to reveal rather than to conceal his identity. We are to make him known everywhere as the divine Savior.

Jesus did not come to be a celebrity in the shallow sense of a Hollywood "superstar." His fame was a natural result of his person, words, and deeds. He did not seek notoriety; it sought him.

16

The Mission of the King

Scripture Reading: Mark 1:35–39

A popular subject for books, movies, and television is the spy thriller in which the secret agent is sent on a top-secret mission. From James Bond to "Mission Impossible" the excitement, intrigue, and danger of a vital assignment, involving national security, captures our imaginations.

No one has ever engaged in a mission so daring, so bold, or so vital as that undertaken by the Lord Jesus Christ. He infiltrated behind enemy lines to rescue the hostages of sin.

I. **Prayer Is the Preparation for It (v. 35)**
    A. Here at the outset of his ministry Jesus prepares himself for his assignment from the Father. He seeks, even before the sun is up, a solitary place where he can receive inner strength for his task by fellowshiping with his heavenly Father.
    B. Christ did not feel ready to embark on his mission until he had prepared for it by meditation and intercession. How can we dare to approach our work for the Lord without bathing each day in prayer?

II. **Popularity Is the Enemy of It (vv. 36, 37)**
    A. Each time Jesus is seen seeking solitude in Mark's Gospel it relates to his struggle with temptation regarding his messiahship. His continued popularity with the crowds depended upon his conforming to their notions of a Savior, which were contrary to God's.

B. When popularity tempts us to compromise our convictions, we are in danger of forfeiting our status as missionaries of Christ. The desire for the praise of men is an enemy of our holy calling.

III. Preaching Is the Heart of It (vv. 38, 39a)

A. The message Jesus proclaimed was the good news that God's salvation was at hand. By turning back to God in Christ, Jesus' hearers could participate in the coming of the kingdom.

B. Even as preaching took precedence over miracles and healing in the ministry of Jesus, the proclamation is still the heart of any missionary enterprise. Unless the gospel is being preached, our hospitals, orphanages, and schools are but a temporary ministry.

IV. Power Is the Corollary to It (v. 39b)

A. The miracles of our Lord were not simply a means of ministering to people's needs. They were performed as a sign that what Jesus preached was true.

B. When God sends us a mission, he equips us to perform it. Though we do not perform miracles, we still have the Holy Spirit's power, especially to drive away Satan as people accept Christ.

He who gave us the Great Commission was himself the first missionary. He was given the all-but-impossible mission of saving rebellious, sinful man, yet he accomplished our salvation.

17

The Compassion of the King

Scripture Reading: Mark 1:40–45

There are people who so identify with others who are in pain that they actually experience sympathy pains. Such folks are compassionate in the literal sense of being able to "suffer with" others.

The most compassionate person who ever lived was, of course, Jesus of Nazareth. In the gospels we see him moved with compassion, overcome with another's grief, weeping over Jerusalem.

In this passage we see the compassion of the King for the most pitiful of all outcasts, a leper. From this incident we see that our Lord's pity

I. Is Stirred by Suffering (vv. 40, 41)

    A. The picture of this poor, unfortunate creature limping to Jesus is a vivid one. His twisted frame kneels down (who knows at what cost in pain) before our Lord as he makes his petition of faith. The great heart of Jesus goes out to him; and not his heart only but his hand as well.

    B. We have a Savior who is not cold and indifferent to the suffering of God's children. His compassion and will are stirred by our needs.

II. Is Manifested in Ministry (v. 42)

    A. Our Savior is not one of those who weep crocodile tears and cluck their tongues at the misfortune of others, yet never lift a finger to help. He demonstrated his concern in a tangible way.

B. We do not have Jesus' ability to heal everyone who comes to us or to supply the need of every person with whom we come into contact. But we can do something about someone's suffering, even if we cannot do everything about everyone's problems; even if we can only offer a listening ear or promise to pray for them.

III. Is an Opportunity for Homage (vv. 43, 44)

A. The Mosaic law made provision for those whom God had healed to thank and praise him. There was a procedure for examination and a specific offering of thanks for healing.

B. Anytime the compassion of Jesus results in our deliverance, whether it be from illness, or depression, or fear, or sin, that is an occasion for bearing witness to others of the love and power of God.

IV. Is the Cause of Complications (v. 45)

A. By showing compassion to the leper, Jesus' life was complicated. His ministry was made more difficult. But that did not stop him from "getting his hands dirty" helping others.

B. Involvement in the problems of others is a messy business. We run the risk of making trouble for ourselves, but we must put aside any thought of personal inconvenience if we would imitate our Savior.

We do not, by nature, have the compassion of the King. He must give it to us, for we have become hardened by the plight of the poor, the oppressed, the infirm.

We are so overwhelmed by the magnitude of pain and suffering in our world that we find it difficult to feel sorry for individual sufferers. Pray that God may remove the calluses from our hearts.

Part 3

The Sayings
of the Savior

18

The Bread of Life

Scripture Reading: John 6:51

One of the consequences of the fall was the curse: "In the sweat of thy face shalt thou eat bread" (Gen. 3:19). We must toil and labor for our food. Yet the bread does not last, and we must soon eat again.

Nor does this bread satisfy our deeper hungers. We long for bread that will fill our souls and satisfy our spirits. There is such bread and it is Jesus Christ himself.

I. **The Bread Came Down from Heaven**
   A. After Jesus fed the five thousand the crowds sought him, not out of full hearts but on account of their full bellies. He urged them to labor for enduring rather than perishing bread.
   B. The people thought of the manna that fell from heaven in Moses' time. But Jesus said the manna was not the Bread of Life, for those who ate it died.

II. **The Bread Confers Eternal Life**
   A. The statement about living forever is both conditional and universal. It depends on whether or not one eats it. Those who eat of that Bread, regardless of who they are, have eternal life.
   B. Thus there is also a promise for us, because the Bread of Life is still available to any and all who would partake of it.

III. The Bread Consists of Christ Himself

    A. While this statement shocks us as cannibalism, those who first heard it understood it. They had a background of eating the remains of animal sacrifices offered to God as a way of being nourished by the life of the deity.

    B. In the case of Christ, the giving of his flesh refers both to his atoning death and to his resurrection life available to us.

Jesus said that he came that his disciples "might have life, and that they might have it more abundantly" (John 10:10). He is the Bread who supplies this life, a spiritual life, which is full and free and satisfying, as well as never ending.

Have you partaken of this Living Bread? His offer for us to dine on the Bread of Life is still open. Won't you accept that "dinner invitation" today?

19

The Light of the World

The men of a certain Indian tribe rise early every morning to perform an ancient ceremony that causes the sun to come up. They believe that if they failed to perform this ritual, they would plunge the world into utter darkness.

Without sunlight, life on this planet would quickly cease to exist. Even more vital to us is that true Light on whom our spiritual life depends. Without Christ all humankind would be doomed to grope about forever in the cold darkness of sin.

I. Jesus Claimed to Be the Light of the World

    A. Our Lord made this claim during the Feast of Tabernacles, which began with a candlelight service in the temple. The ceremony, called "The Illumination of the Temple," took place on the first night of the festival in the Court of the Women.

    B. With this event fresh in the minds of the people, Jesus came to this same court and announced that he was the real Light.

II. There Is a Condition to Enjoying This Light

    A. Before the Light of Christ can benefit us, we must become his followers. We must go where the Light goes or be left in darkness.

    B. Have you followed Christ in salvation, in baptism, in church membership, and in discipleship? The closer you walk with him the greater the Light you will have!

III. The Consequence of Following Jesus Is Having the Light of Life
   A. Although we live in an age of scientific enlighten-ment, we find ourselves in one of the darkest peri-ods of history morally and spiritually. Violent crime, drug abuse, sexual perversion, broken homes, politi-cal corruption, international terrorism—these and countless other moral cancers eat away at our social life.
   B. Such darkness can be pierced only by the Light of Christ. Only those who follow him have a candle to illumine their way in the world.

The old gospel song, "The Light of the World Is Jesus" has been omitted from some modern hymnals. This is regrettable because it is a wonderful reminder that Jesus is the only true source of Light in a world engulfed by the night of sin and death.

20

The Scandalous Claim

Periodically the religious world is rocked by scandal. From the fictional Elmer Gantry to his all-too-real-life counterparts, some preachers' behavior shocks and offends even the lost world. Clearly such misconduct is morally reprehensible and is even more odious to God than it is to people.

Strange to say, it is also possible to scandalize others by doing the *right* thing. When society's values are distorted, it will be outraged by truth and goodness. Our Lord himself caused a scandal when he made some profound claims.

I. Jesus Is Messiah (vv. 56, 57)
   A. What did Jesus mean when he said that Abraham had seen his day? The Jews took him to mean that he had been born before Abraham died. Some think he meant that Abraham looked down from heaven on the nativity and rejoiced.
   B. Most likely, however, Abraham foresaw in prophecy the coming of Messiah and rejoiced in that promise (Gen. 12:3; 15:8–21).

II. Jesus Is Eternal (v. 58)
   A. The Jews asked Jesus if he was claiming to have existed since the time of Abraham. He was claiming more than that: He said he existed *before* Abraham—indeed, before everything.
   B. The New Testament is not at all reticent about asserting the eternal existence of Christ. Such pas-

sages as John 1:1, 14; Colossians 1:15–17 and
Hebrews 13:8 speak boldly and clearly of the pre-
existence of Christ.

III. Jesus Is God (vv. 58, 59)

    A. By saying "I am," Christ was not only claiming eternal existence, he was attributing to himself the divine name. Since it was considered blasphemy even to pronounce this taboo word, to appropriate it for oneself was so unthinkable as to be shocking in the extreme.

    B. They could not accept the Lord's claim as true, so it was not surprising that they attempted to stone him in accordance with the law of Leviticus 24:16.

Many are still scandalized that one whom they consider to be a mere man would make such an outlandish claim. They could accept him as a great religious founder on a par with other teachers of righteousness. But the assertion to be the Messiah, the eternal Son of God, continues to scandalize most of the world.

Does Jesus' claim offend you? Or are you ready to accept it and admit that Jesus is precisely who he claimed to be? Do not trip over the stumbling block of our Lord's rightful claim.

21

The Doorway to Life

Scripture Reading: John 10:9, 10

In the old story of the lady and the tiger a young man is forced to choose between two closed doors. Behind one is a beautiful princess whom he may take as his bride; behind the other crouches death at the jaws of a man-eating tiger.

Must all our life-and-death choices be blind ones? We may be thankful that when it comes to our eternal welfare, the doorway to life is clearly marked. Jesus is the entrance into a life of

I. **Salvation (v. 9a)**
   A. *Saved* is one of the great words of the New Testament. It contains the ideas of wholeness and healing, of forgiveness and restoration, of blessing and victory.
   B. There is only one way into the benefits of liberty, peace, and happiness. Unless we enter by and through Christ, we cannot enter into life at all.

II. **Security (v. 9b)**
   A. The freedom to go in and out, and to do so in complete safety and security, means that one is a citizen of a country that is at peace and in which law and order prevail (*see* Ps. 121:8).
   B. In Jesus we have perfect safety and security. While this does not guarantee us immunity from physical harm, it does mean that, whatever happens to us, we are in God's hands.

III. Satisfaction (v. 9c)

A. The finding of pasture is a beautiful picture of needs being met and hungers being satisfied. Jesus is the doorway to that which fills our souls with spiritual sustenance.

B. Millions feel like the Rolling Stones' song of the 1960s: "I Can't Get No Satisfaction." We need only to pass through the right door to find a life that is truly fulfilling.

IV. Sufficiency (v. 10)

A. The abundant life is one of bounty, of overflowing, of supersufficiency. We long for vitality and hope, excitement and enthusiasm, purpose and meaning.

B. In Christ we find that we can exchange our dull, gray, drab existence for a life that is really worth living.

This matter of which door to choose is no trivial one. The issues are not those of a game-show contestant who stands to win a refrigerator! It is more serious even than the case of the lady and the tiger, for we face a choice between a life and a death that are both *eternal*.

22

The Good Shepherd

Scripture Reading: John 10:11–16

It is difficult for most of us to identify with the image of a sheepherder tending his flock. The closest we come to sheep is wearing a wool sweater or eating roast lamb or reading "Little Bo-Peep" to children!

Once we are able to go back in time and understand the background of Jesus' words in this passage, the analogy becomes very meaningful. The Good Shepherd, says Jesus,

I. Gives His Life for His Sheep (vv. 11–13)
   A. There were some occupational hazards to sheepherding. Wild animals such as wolves, lions, and even bears were a constant danger. Continual vigilance was required of a shepherd.
   B. Only a good shepherd who really cared about the flock would put their welfare above his own safety. Jesus gave his life for us, his sheep.

II. Knows and Is Known by His Sheep (vv. 14, 15)
   A. Sheep soon learn to recognize the voice of their shepherd and will absolutely not follow a stranger. Yet if their shepherd calls them by name, they will stop grazing to obey him.
   B. Be assured that the Good Shepherd knows your name. If you belong to him you can recognize his voice when he speaks to you. But do you always obey when he does?

III. Gathers Together All His Sheep (v. 16)

    A. It was not unusual for a shepherd to have more than one flock. Though they might be separated for purposes of pasturing, they came together at night into one sheepfold.

    B. Christ has brought us together, people of all races and backgrounds, whether Jews or Gentiles, into one fold (literally one "flock"). Whatever ecclesiastical fold we are in, we who know the Good Shepherd are part of his one great flock.

Without Jesus we are "as sheep not having a shepherd" (Mark 6:34). Sheep without a shepherd are lost, helpless, and vulnerable. They cannot find pasture by themselves and are easy prey to predators. So are men and women without the Good Shepherd to tend their souls.

23

The Resurrection and the Life

Scripture Reading: John 11:23–27

Ever since the time of Job men have been asking, "If a man die, shall he live again?" (Job 14:14). That question still haunts us, and recent studies have examined the experiences of people who were pronounced clinically dead but were subsequently resuscitated.

Jesus Christ not only taught that there was a resurrection, he claimed to be it! In this passage our Lord made three astounding statements about himself in this regard.

  I. To the Dying, Jesus Is the Resurrection (v. 25)
   - A. When Jesus arrived on the scene, his friend had already been dead at least four days (v. 17). Mourning was perhaps greater in those days because there was little more than a glimmer of hope for a future life (Job 19:25–27; Pss. 16:9–11; 73:23, 24). Many, notably the Sadducees, denied even the possibility of resurrection.
   - B. To the dead and dying, Jesus offers the promise of deliverance from death and the blessed prospect of everlasting life.

  II. To the Living, Jesus Is the Life (v. 26)
   - A. The living, no less than the dying, need what only Jesus can offer. Those who trust in him will never really die. Physical death will be only a transition to a higher plane of existence.

   B. Some have seen here a reference to the return of
    Christ. They point out that to those who "are alive
    and remain" (1 Thess. 4:15), he will be life, as they
    are translated into heaven without seeing death.
    (Compare with Phil. 1:21.)

III. To the Believing, Jesus Is the Christ (v. 27)
   A. Before he can be either resurrection or life to us, we
    must come to believe with Martha that Jesus is "the
    Christ, the Son of God."
   B. Faith in Christ is the key that unlocks the door into
    life everlasting. Have you believed in him as your
    personal Lord and Savior?

What a tremendous difference it makes in our hearts and lives
to know that in Jesus we have the sure hope of resurrection unto
life eternal. The words of this text are backed up by the resurrection of Jesus from the dead.

24

The Highway to Heaven

Scripture Reading: John 14:6

It was said in the ancient world that all roads led to Rome. The Roman Empire boasted some of the best roads ever built. Their highway system held the empire together and facilitated transportation, communication, and conquest. They were a boon to pilgrims too.

Spiritually speaking we are all on a journey. Hopefully we want to get to heaven eventually. Which road do we take? In John 14:6 Jesus tells us that he is the highway to heaven. Notice

I. **The Direction of the Highway ("I am the way")**
   A. It was the persistent prodding of Thomas that provoked our Lord's tremendous words. There is nothing wrong with asking questions. Thomas felt lost and wisely asked directions.
   B. Only Jesus can point us in the right direction. His life and teachings, his death and resurrection, are our guideposts and he himself is the highway.

II. **A Description of the Highway ("I am . . . the truth")**
   A. Many good and wise people have told us some truth. None but Jesus ever embodied it perfectly. He is truth incarnate.
   B. Biblical writers and secular thinkers alike sought truth, though with differing success. But when truth was finally revealed in its totality, it looked like Jesus.

III. The Destination of the Highway ("I am . . . the life")
   A. The most important consideration in choosing a road is where it leads. Its surface, width, and scenery are secondary issues.
   B. Following Jesus takes us to our desired destination: heaven. The byways of sin may offer comfort and diversions, but they lead us farther and farther away from our desired goal.

In its early days, the Christian faith was known simply as "the Way." There are many ways but only one right Way. Is your life headed the wrong way? Then exit now. Take the next off-ramp from sin and get on the highway to heaven!

25

The Cultivation of the Church

Scripture Reading: John 15:1–10

Television commercials are rarely popular features of that medium. However, one cereal advertisement that has captured the imagination of the viewing audience stars a chorus of animated raisins singing "I Heard It Through the Grapevine."

Jesus used the luxuriant fertility of the grapevine to symbolize his relationship to his church. Like the grapevine, the church requires careful cultivation if it is to be fruitful. This nurture

I. **Derives from the Love of God, the Heavenly Husbandman (vv. 1, 2)**
   A. Most likely Jesus spoke these words during the Passover meal, possibly at one of those points when the fruit of the vine was served. Grapevines require a great deal of care and drastic pruning to reach their full potential.
   B. God, the divine vinedresser, knows how to cultivate the church so that it will bear much fruit.

II. **Draws Upon the Life of Christ, the Veritable Vine (vv. 4, 5)**
   A. The branches of a grapevine draw their nourishment from the stem and root system from which flow the vital sap of life. If they become severed from their stem they wither and die quickly.
   B. A Christian who is relying on his own finite strength and resources cannot bear good fruit.

Indeed he cannot long survive without partaking of the life of Christ.

III. Depends on the Loyalty of Disciples, the Believing Branches (vv. 4–10)

A. The cultivation of the church depends on our abiding in Christ. Whatever else this means, it certainly includes constant contact and fellowship with Christ through prayer, Bible study, and a holy walk.

B. If we fail to maintain this living link with Christ, we will become like the wild, uncultivated vineyard to which the prophets likened apostate Israel (Isa. 5:1–7; Jer. 2:21). A grapevine left to itself dissipates its strength in overrunning the ground with fruitless branches (Ezek. 15; 19:10; Hos. 10:1; Ps. 80:8).

The church is privileged to be part of the vine of Christ. We are called upon literally to "branch out" to others, bearing the fruit of souls won to Christ and ministry performed to those in need.

Part 4

The Ministry
of the Savior

26

The Confident Christian

Scripture Reading: Matthew 10:24–33

Too many Christians live timid lives, afraid to take risks, fearful of the future. They miss out on life because they live in mortal dread of pain, suffering, and disappointment.

As Jesus taught his disciples, fear does not become a follower of his. A cowardly life is no life at all. On the contrary, the confident Christian

I. Recognizes the Reality of Evil (vv. 24–28)
    A. Jesus did not deny the fact of danger. Christians are not promised immunity from harm nor exemption from persecution.
    B. Jesus did affirm the certainty of victory. Though we are called upon to suffer, or even to die, the cause of Christ will triumph. This is no shallow optimism, no Pollyanna glibness, but real, courageous faith.

II. Reposes in the Reign of God (vv. 29–31)
    A. The power of evil, though real, is limited. Harm reaches us only by God's permission. (Compare with Job 1:12.)
    B. The love and power of God, on the other hand, are infinite. God's care extends even to the "insignificant" sparrows, and not even one of them can perish unless God allows it. How much more does God watch over us?

III. Remembers the Reward of Christ (vv. 32, 33)

    A. Our sufferings for Christ will be rewarded. If we refuse to allow the threat (or even the fact) of persecution to intimidate us into silence, we shall be amply compensated by Jesus' commendation.

    B. The only thing a Christian should fear is displeasing the Lord. That fear should cancel out every other. Fight fear with fear!

When we stop to think of it: What *we* live in cringing fear of as witnesses for Christ is not the death or torture that some believers have been asked to suffer but only an occasional door slammed in our faces. We ought to be ashamed of our cowardice!

27

The Great Confession

Scripture Reading: Matthew 16:13–20

The world has seen many revolutionary ideas: Copernicus's affirmation that the earth revolves around the sun, Thomas Jefferson's insistence that "all men are created equal," Einstein's theories of relativity.

Yet as radical as these concepts were, they cannot hold a candle to the confession of a simple fisherman nearly two thousand years ago. Simon Peter's statement of faith rocked the world to its foundations.

I. **The Location of the Confession (v. 13a)**
   A. Peter's confession was made at Caesarea Philippi, a pagan area named after Augustus Caesar and Philip the Tetrarch. It was noted for its pagan idol worship of nature gods.
   B. We can confess Christ anywhere. Such a profession hallows even formerly unholy ground.

II. **The Interrogation of the Disciples (v. 13b)**
   A. This confession was prompted by questions that Jesus asked. Socrates of old had employed this method of teaching so successfully that it is still known by his name.
   B. Jesus, the Master Teacher, used many methods to educate his disciples. By asking them questions, he caused them to think.

III. The Misconceptions of the People (v. 14)

A. The disciples repeated to Jesus the opinions of others. Some of these were superstitious, some were fanciful, some were inadequate, but all were erroneous.

B. Secondhand convictions and a hearsay faith are always unsatisfactory. Our knowledge of Christ must be based on our personal experience and understanding.

IV. The Affirmation of the Spokesman (vv. 15, 16)

A. Characteristically, it was Peter who spoke for the whole group. Not that all of them necessarily agreed (for instance, Judas).

B. Peter's affirmation showed insight and comprehension, a *revelation* from God which none had yet put into words. It was the greatest confession ever made.

V. The Approbation of the Lord (v. 17)

A. Jesus congratulated Peter on being so blessed. He commended his sensitivity to God's voice, which enabled him to "pick up on" this tremendous truth.

B. Anyone who makes this same confession, though it is no longer original, still does it through the inspiration of God's Spirit. Moreover, such a one shares Peter's blessedness for doing it.

VI. The Foundation of the Church (v. 18)

A. This great confession (or, rather, the one whom Peter confessed) was to form the basis of the church. The church was called into existence to share the truth of Peter's confession with the world.

B. Any so-called church or denomination that denies the content of Peter's words or neglects to proclaim it to the lost is, whatever good it does otherwise, built on a false and shaky foundation.

VII. The Proclamation of the Gospel (vv. 19, 20)
A. Preaching the truth of Peter's confession is the key that unlocks the gates of hell to let the prisoners out as well as the gates of heaven to let the repentant in.
B. For that time, Jesus forbade the disciples to reveal his identity, that they might proclaim it the more boldly at the proper time. That time has long since arrived, and we are to spread the gospel around the world.

Whom do *you* say that Jesus is? Do you share Peter's conviction? Or are you one of those many who give an inadequate or a secondhand answer to this most important question in the world?

28

The Messiah's Metamorphosis

Scripture Reading: Matthew 17:1–9

This mysterious occurrence, recorded in all three synoptic Gospels, is commonly called "the Transfiguration." The Greek word is *metamorphosis*, "an alteration in physical form." To obtain all the details, Matthew's account must be supplemented by that of Mark (9:2–9) and Luke (9:28–36). The main elements of this event are

I. The Transformation in a Vision (vv. 2, 9)

    A. While the "inner circle" of three disciples looked on, Jesus' face and clothing became radiant with a brilliant white light. This is reminiscent of the Shechinah glory of God's presence in the Old Testament.

    B. This event has been described as the divinity of Christ shining through his humanity.

    C. Jesus' designation of this occurrence as a "vision" in no way implies that it was only a dream. It implies that those present were enabled to behold something that was normally not visible.

II. The Conversation with the Visitors (vv. 3, 4)

    A. Why were these two particular individuals present? One suggestion is that Moses represents the law as Elijah does the prophets. Another is that Moses

stands for believers who die in the Lord, while Elijah stands for those who will be translated without seeing death.
   B. What was the subject of their conversation? Only Luke (9:31) tells us that the topic under discussion was Christ's imminent death at Jerusalem.
   C. What was behind Peter's inane suggestion? Perhaps he wanted to freeze time and hold on to this "mountaintop experience." He seems to have mistakenly placed Moses, Elijah, and Jesus on the same level.

III. **The Command of the Voice (vv. 5–9)**
   A. The voice of God spoke from a bright "cloud." The cloud of God's glory is prominent in the Old Testament, particularly during the Exodus. It indicated God's presence.
   B. The voice commended Christ and commanded the disciples to listen to him. God's voice had also affirmed his pleasure in his Son at Jesus' baptism (Matt. 3:17).
   C. Jesus dispelled the disciples' fear and charged them to keep quiet about this mysterious event until after his resurrection. The vanishing of Moses and Elijah served to correct both of Peter's errors.

This miraculous occurrence was a kind of "sneak preview" of Christ's second advent. As the glory of his deity pierced the veil of his humanity, so shall he appear "when the Son of man shall come in his glory, and all the holy angels with him" (Matt. 25:31).

29

The Cost of Discipleship

Scripture Reading: Luke 9:23–26

One of the classics of Christian literature is Dietrich Bonhoeffer's *The Cost of Discipleship*. As an outspoken opponent of Naziism, Bonhoeffer, a German Lutheran pastor, was martyred for his stand.

There is a price to be paid for following Jesus. In our Scripture for today Christ calculates for us the cost of discipleship.

I. **Its Down Payment Is Self-denial (v. 23a)**
    A. Self-denial is more than abstention from some pleasure. It is infinitely more than giving up meat for Lent. To deny oneself is to disown, to renounce our very selves and our will in favor of God and his will.
    B. That is not to say that self-denial is the same as asceticism. Hair shirts and harsh penance are no substitute for disclaiming all rights to self-determination (1 Cor. 6:19, 20).

II. **Its Daily Expense Is Self-sacrifice (v. 23b)**
    A. Cross bearing is not burden bearing. Worries and problems are not the crosses we have to bear. In fact, Jesus does not want us to bear burdens (Matt. 11:28, 30).
    B. Cross bearing is dying to self. It is not the cross's weight but its significance that matters. One who carried a cross was a condemned man. Christians have died to self to live for Christ.

III. Its Decisive Price Is Self-submission (v. 23c)

    A. Following Christ means more than following his teachings or even his example. We might do that with any great religious teacher.

    B. Following Christ means going where he leads us. When he spoke these words he was on his way to Calvary. We must be willing to say, "Wherever he leads I'll go."

IV. Its Destined Payoff Is Self-fulfillment (v. 24)

    A. There is a current craze obsessed with finding fulfillment through the "human-potential" movement. From ESP to T.M. and from subliminal tapes to scientology people are seeking the true self buried deep in the psyche.

    B. Fulfillment is not found in ourselves but in Christ. If discipleship has a high price, it pays even greater dividends. The reward of following Christ is nothing less than life itself: abundant, eternal, and fulfilling life.

Salvation is a free gift of God's grace, yet it costs us everything. In this paradox lies the secret of discipleship—and of happiness.

30

God Helps Those Who . . .

Scripture Reading: Mark 10:46–52

The old saying "God helps those who help themselves" is, contrary to popular opinion, not found in the Bible. There are some scriptural endings to that phrase, however, in thought if not in these exact words. For God helps those who

I. Profess Their Need of Christ (vv. 46, 47)
   A. Bartimaeus was both blind and poor. He was dependent on the compassion and charity of others for his survival. Pride was a luxury he could not afford.
   B. Bartimaeus used his remaining faculties to the utmost. He could hear and speak. When he heard that Jesus was coming, he cried out for his help.
   C. Bartimaeus did not wait for complete understanding before calling on the Lord. He called Jesus the "son of David," which was a true but inadequate ascription.
   D. Do not let pride, self-pity, or imperfect knowledge keep you from admitting your need of God's help in Christ.

II. Persevere in the Prayer of Faith (vv. 48–51)
   A. Bartimaeus prayed for help. True, his cry was not couched in liturgical language nor offered in a church, but it was a prayer nonetheless.
   B. The onlookers interfered with the blind man's prayer. Instead of saying "Amen" they told him to

keep quiet and conduct himself in a more respect-
able manner in Jesus' presence.
   C. The beggar did not let the criticism of others stop
      him from coming to Jesus. He was not concerned
      with what people thought of him but with obtaining
      God's help.
   D. Are you persistent in your prayers? Do you keep
      calling on the Lord until he answers, even if people
      call you a "fanatic" for doing so? Is your faith
      strong enough to persevere in prayer?

III. Propose to Follow Christ in Discipleship (v. 52)
   A. Bartimaeus became a follower of Christ once his
      sight was restored. He did not settle for mere physi-
      cal healing.
   B. Jesus' way became Bartimaeus's way. Christ said,
      "Go thy way," but he followed Jesus.
   C. Why do you want Christ to answer your prayers?
      So you can follow Christ and serve him better? Or
      are your motives selfish in wanting to use your
      answered prayers sinfully?

We may well say to this poor, handicapped man, "Move over,
Bartimaeus. Is there room on that road for me? For I, too, am a
blind beggar in need of the Master's healing touch."

31

Anatomy of a Grateful Heart

Scripture Reading: Luke 17:11–19

"As long as you have your health you have everything" goes an old saying. We take good health for granted until it is taken away from us. In this passage, ten men were healed of a tragic, catastrophic, terminal illness, but only one showed any gratitude for the precious gift of restored health. A grateful heart

I. Turns Back to Glorify God (v. 15)
   A. All ten lepers were healed, but only one returned to praise God for his healing. Ironically, he was a Samaritan, returning to thank the Jew who had healed him.
   B. The Samaritan might have waited for official confirmation from the priests before offering thanks to Jesus. He might have glorified God as he went. He might have rushed back into the bosom of his family first—but he stopped to turn back.
   C. He glorified God with a loud voice. Do we thank God for answered prayer as loudly as we prayed for an answer?

II. Falls Down to Worship Christ (vv. 16–18)
   A. Worship must include thanksgiving or it is incomplete.
   B. God's blessings come to us through his Son.
   C. Jesus was not surprised that this man returned to give thanks. Rather, he was dismayed that the other

nine failed to do so. Gratitude is not some rare, optional virtue but the common duty of all men.

III. Rises Up to Live in Wholeness (v. 19)
- A. Jesus' words here are not merely a reminder of the leper's physical healing. It was an extra, spiritual blessing, an additional work of grace.
- B. When we are properly thankful for God's blessings we obtain yet another blessing. Gratitude endows our lives with a spiritual wholeness that overshadows even the material blessings of God.

We must not wait until Thanksgiving to give thanks to God. The attitude of gratitude must become the habit of our daily lives.

32

Prayer—Contrition or Congratulation?

Scripture Reading: Luke 18:9–14

The Bible says that "men ought always to pray, and not to faint" (Luke 18:1). But can prayer be wrong? Is there such a thing as a bad prayer?

Our Lord told us that there is a right way and a wrong way to pray. It depends on whether our prayer is an act of contrition or an exercise in self-congratulation. In his parable of the Pharisee and the publican, we observe three things about prayer.

I. **The Similarities in the Two Prayers**
   A. Both men went to the same place to pray. It is not necessary to go to a house of worship to pray, but many people feel closer to God there. Yet simply being in God's house does not guarantee that our prayers will be heard.
   B. Both men came for the same purpose. At least it would seem so from all appearances. Both men claimed that they were there to pray and to worship God.
   C. Both men had made the same preparation. Prior to coming to the temple both men had seriously examined their lives, although they came to opposite conclusions.

II. **The Standards of the Two Prayers**
   A. The Pharisee compared himself to others, especially others who seemed to him to be more sinful

than himself. He looked around instead of looking up. His eyes were on his fellow worshipers and not on God.

B. The publican compared himself to God's Word. He knew that he might find others compared to whom even a despised tax-collector would look good. But measured against the absolute standard of God's Word, he knew himself to be a miserable sinner.

C. We cannot pray rightly if we are busy criticizing the people in the other pews. Even if they were "worse" sinners than we are, that would not justify us before God.

III. The Sequels to the Two Prayers

A. The Pharisee came away unchanged. He had made no important decision, had had no real encounter with God, had grasped no new truth. He had not been praying to God but "with himself."

B. The publican went away a different man. As he confessed his sin and repented of it, his life was turned around, and he began a new relationship with God as a forgiven sinner.

C. The true measure of our prayer life is the result it produces in us. If we come away from church self-satisfied and self-righteous, we have not really met with God in prayer.

The purpose of prayer is not to bend the will of God to our will, but ours to his. It is not God's mind we seek to change in prayer, but our attitudes.

33

Jesus' Desire for His Disciples

Scripture Reading: John 17:20–26

There are few countries whose history has not been marred by civil war. There is no more tragic picture than that of a fractured nation whose severed halves have turned against each other in mutual self-destruction—unless it be a church torn by strife.

In his Gethsemane prayer Jesus asked the Father that the disciples—present and future—might be one. It was and is Jesus' desire for his church to be marked by harmony rather than hostility and friendship instead of factionalism. He prayed for

I. **A Perfect Unity (vv. 21a, 22b, 23a)**
    A. A oneness like that found in the Trinity is the perfect pattern of unity.
    B. We must go beyond mere organizational union to the genuine oneness of organic unity. Only the bond of holy love can forge such an inward togetherness.

II. **An Effective Testimony (vv. 21b, 23b)**
    A. The only way the world can come to know Christ is to see him in the lives of believers. Our walk must not belie our talk.
    B. The sorry spectacle of a bickering church negates our talk of love and oneness. A sweet fellowship is so rare that it requires a supernatural explanation!

III. **A Glorious Intimacy (vv. 22a, 24)**
    A. Jesus also desires that we share his glory. He wants us to be with him so that we may gaze on his glory.

B. Doubtless there is an eschatalogical element in this thought, but we do not have to wait until the second coming or until we die to behold Christ's glory. When we walk in fellowship with him we fulfill his desire for a glorious intimacy with us.

IV. A Divine Charity (v. 26)

A. Most of all Jesus wants us to love each other with the same kind of *agape* love that the heavenly Father has for his Son.

B. *Agape* is sometimes translated "charity." It does not mean almsgiving, however, but that attitude of goodwill which could show itself through philanthropic causes.

Has it dawned on you that you have the power to grant Jesus' prayer? How can we who claim to be his disciples squabble over petty concerns when we remember his agonized prayer in the Garden of Gethsemane for our unity on the very eve of his crucifixion?

Part 5

The Salvation
of the Savior

34

The King Has Come

Scripture Reading: Matthew 21:1–11

Today is Palm Sunday, the day we commemorate our Lord's triumphal entry into Jerusalem. Why should we celebrate such a holiday? What significance does this event have that would justify its inclusion in the Christian calendar?

Palm Sunday means that the King of kings has come to us, offering to bring in the long-awaited and longed-for kingdom of God. This passage tells us not only *that* the King has come, but also *how* and *why* he has come. When Jesus rode into Jerusalem it was

I. In Fulfillment of Prophecy (v. 4)

A. The prophecy referred to is Zechariah 9:9, a passage from the apocalyptic section of that book. In chapter 14 the prophet went on to predict that the Messiah would begin his ride from the Mount of Olives.

B. Jesus fulfilled these prophecies—and hundreds of others—to the letter. In fact, fulfilled prophecy is one of the strong arguments for the inspiration of the Bible and the truth of the gospel.

II. In Humility of Person (v. 5a)

A. Meekness is not weakness. Meekness is the trait of a gentleman: one who is both gentle and manly, kind and forgiving, quiet and unassuming. Though a meek person may become angry, he is never petty and vengeful.

B. Meekness in outward behavior is due to mildness in one's inward disposition. It is the result of an attitude directed first toward God, then toward others. Meekness is the opposite of today's craze for self-assertiveness. Jesus is the embodiment of meekness and humility.

III. In Peacefulness of Purpose (v. 5b)

A. Besides fulfilling prophecy, Jesus' ride into Jerusalem on a donkey symbolized peace. In peacetime rulers often rode on beasts of burden such as mules or donkeys, horses being reserved for war.

B. By choosing this humble mode of transport, our Lord made it clear that he was coming as the Prince of peace, not as a warrior to defeat Rome.

In Revelation 19:11 Christ is seen returning mounted on a white charger to make war on his enemies. If we reject him as the Prince of peace, we shall have to face him as Judge and King of kings.

35

Three Reactions
to the Crucifixion

Scripture Reading: Matthew 27:35–61

Just as there were three basic responses to Jesus' birth (typified by the Magi, Herod, and the priests and scribes), so there was a threefold reaction to his death. In the faces of those who stood at the foot of the cross, we see a mirror of today's attitudes.

I. Some Are Cold and Callous (vv. 35–37)

A. The hardened soldiers crucified our Lord without emotion. They sat down to watch his agony with the same indifference with which one might observe a mouse being tormented by a cat.

B. Their only interest was in exploiting his death to obtain his meager possessions. So insensitive were they to the spectacle of Christ's agony, they amused themselves with gambling for his garment.

C. Is your heart so hard that the crucifixion of Christ cannot move you to sorrow? Is your only interest in his death what you can get out of it?

II. Some Are Moved to Mockery (vv. 38–47)

A. One of the thieves only cared about his own suffering—no matter that he deserved it or that Jesus was innocent. He jeered at Jesus for not using his power to save himself and the thieves.

B. The passersby sadistically added to his suffering. Incredibly, they would deny him relief for the sake of nothing but their curiosity.

C. The religious leaders delighted in casting his claims back in his face. They wanted revenge for all the times he had shown them up for the hypocrites they were.

III. Some Are Stirred to Sympathy (vv. 48–61)

A. An unnamed observer sought to ease Jesus' suffering by the administration of a pain-killing drug.

B. The centurion was sensitive enough to perceive something extraordinary about the way Christ faced suffering and death.

C. The women did what they could, even if it was only to stand by helplessly from a distance and later remain at the graveside.

D. Joseph of Arimathea used his wealth to provide for the body of our Lord.

What is your reaction to Christ's death on the cross for you? Is it one of cold indifference, cruel mockery, or sensitive adoration?

36

Unsolved Mystery or Undeniable Miracle?

Scripture Reading: John 20:1–18

A popular television program dramatizes police cases in which authorities have been unable to solve mysterious crimes. Occasionally viewers have been able to offer information that led to the arrest of perpetrators or the location of missing persons.

Some skeptics consider the events following Jesus' crucifixion to be an unsolved mystery, dismissing the one explanation that accounts for all the facts. Let's examine three "clues" in the case.

I. The Unoccupied Tomb (vv. 1–4)

A. No one denies that the tomb was empty. Had the body of Jesus been there, the enemies of Christ could easily have produced it, putting an end to the disciples' claims that he had been raised.

B. Various theories have been advanced to explain the empty tomb apart from the resurrection. Unbelievers have suggested that Jesus' followers went to the wrong tomb, or stole his body, or even that Jesus had only swooned on the cross and revived in the cool dampness of the sepulcher.

C. A little investigation will reveal serious flaws in these explanations. The only solution that fits all the facts is the biblical one: Christ has risen from the dead.

II. The Undisturbed Graveclothes (vv. 5–8)

A. The lifeless body of Jesus had been tightly bound in linen sheets soaked in a hundred pounds of thick, fragrant resins (John 19:39, 40).

B. Both Peter and John saw the collapsed shell of the graveclothes, though only John immediately comprehended their significance. A graverobber would have stolen the body, graveclothes and all. Besides, they had not been cut or unwound and thrown in a heap, but were still neatly arranged in the shape of Jesus' body.

C. There is no logical way to account for this strange phenomenon apart from the bodily resurrection of Christ.

III. The Uncanny Appearances (vv. 11–18)

A. We may take this appearance of Christ to Mary as representative of the dozen or so that the New Testament records.

B. The failure of some to immediately recognize the risen Lord need not trouble us. His appearance may have been altered, either by his ordeal or his resurrection, or both. Also, Mary's eyes were filled with tears, and it was not yet fully light.

C. If the appearances of Christ had been hallucinations, they would not have involved so many people nor multiple senses, including those of sight, hearing, and even touch (1 John 1:1).

Attempting to explain these phenomena without reference to the resurrection involves more difficulties than accepting the New Testament claim that Jesus did indeed rise from the dead. The real unsolved mystery is why so many people refuse to believe it!

37

The Church's Marching Orders

Scripture Reading: Matthew 28:19, 20

Before a battle an army is given its marching orders. The last commands a soldier receives are the ones he is to obey until and unless they are countermanded by subsequent orders. As soldiers of the cross we have been left some "marching orders" by our Captain which have never been revoked. Known as the "Great Commission," these orders are still binding on us. We have been commanded to

I. Make Disciples (v. 19a)
   A. *Go* should be "as you are going," for this is lifestyle evangelism. *Therefore* refers to Jesus' authority, which is the basis of our witness.
   B. The word for *teach* in the King James Version is not the same word so translated in verse 20. Here it is the verb *disciple*. We are to do more than win converts. The real goal of evangelism and missions is to make disciples of every nation.

II. Mark Disciples (v. 19b)
   A. We may think of baptism as a kind of branding. Through this ordinance we are identified with Christ and his church.
   B. Baptism is to be in the name of the Triune God (Acts 8:16, 17; 18:25; 19:1–6). The church is composed of those who are not merely believers, but baptized believers.

III. Mature Disciples (v. 20a)
    A. A disciple is, by definition, a learner. We are to teach those we win. The Christian education program of a church performs a vital function in obeying the Great Commission.
    B. This teaching role is not merely doctrinal or catechetical. We are to train disciples to be doers of the Word and not hearers only (James 1:22).

There is no statute of limitations on our marching orders. They have not been rescinded, nor have we accomplished their objective. We must continue to obey until our Lord returns and we are victorious.

38

If Easter Is a Myth

Scripture Reading: 1 Corinthians 15:12–20

President John F. Kennedy was once asked what he considered to be the greatest convocation of brilliant minds ever assembled at the White House. He replied, "When Thomas Jefferson dined alone."

Yet Jefferson, despite his brilliance (or maybe because it got in the way of faith), rejected miracles, especially the resurrection. Christianity stands or falls on the claim that Jesus Christ has risen from the dead. If Easter is a myth, then

I. Our Message Is Meaningless (v. 14a)

A. *Preaching* here means not "the act of speaking" but what is preached, that is, the content of the sermon.

B. *Vain* means void, empty, ineffectual. The gospel is vacuous, nonsensical gibberish unless Easter celebrates a real, historical event. If Jesus were only a good man, then his words have a hollow ring.

II. Our Faith Is Fruitless (vv. 14b, 17)

A. If Easter is a myth then our faith is misplaced. *Vain* in verse 17 is different than the word so translated in verse 14. Here in verse 17 it means not empty but "useless."

B. Apart from his resurrection, the death of Christ was a failure. By itself it could not atone for our sins, and we have a Savior who cannot save us. Our sins remain unforgiven, and we are doomed to eternal damnation in hell.

III. The Bible Is Baseless (v. 15)

A. If Easter is a myth then the apostles are all liars and the biblical writers have knowingly perjured themselves. In which case we had better reclassify the Bible as religious fiction, disband our churches, and all become secular humanists!

B. If the Bible were not trustworthy it would not have endured through all these centuries as the most beloved and truthful book ever written. If it says Jesus was raised, we may count on it.

IV. Heaven Is Hopeless (vv. 18, 19)

A. If Easter is a myth then we have no hope of a life after death. When you're dead, you're dead, and the hereafter is only a pretty dream.

B. Heaven is a mirage, a hope with no corresponding reality, and Christians are a pitiful bunch of intellectual cripples, limping through life on the crutch of silly superstition—all this if Christ was not raised.

The Christian faith is not helped by removing the resurrection to make it more palatable to modern man. On the contrary, it is destroyed. If Easter is a myth, then so is the Christian faith.

39

The Cosmic Christ

Today's interest in UFOs, "space brothers," and "spirit guides" is nothing new. While we may think of psychic phenomena and alleged extraterrestrial visitations as modern manifestations, a fascination with the "paranormal" is ancient.

One such cult grew up in the area of Colossae in Asia Minor in the first century around supernatural entities and threatened the church there with its heresies. In the process of warning the Colossian Christians against worshiping these beings, the apostle Paul reminded them that Jesus Christ is the Lord of the universe, light years above these so-called lords of the planetary spheres with whom some were flirting. The cosmic Christ

I. Is the Image of God (v. 15a)
    A. The word for *image* here is "icon" and means a likeness, representation, or manifestation of a person. When we look at Christ, we are seeing God.
    B. We do not need intermediary spirits or angels or saints or even his mother Mary to commune with Jesus. He is the divine Son of God "who being the brightness of his glory and the express image of his person" "show[s] us the Father" (Heb. 1:3; John 14:8).

II. Is the Firstborn of Creation (vv. 15b–17)
    A. This expression speaks of Christ's preexistence. "Firstborn" does not mean that he was the first

being to be created, anymore than "begotten" implies that the Father existed before the Son.
   B. This title emphasizes Jesus' right of primogeniture as the divinely appointed "heir of all things" (Heb. 1:2). He is the sphere, agent, and goal of creation, whether of things earthly or heavenly, natural or supernatural. It is he who holds all of creation together.

III. Is the Head of the Church (v. 18)
   A. Jesus' relationship with his church is more personal and intimate than his relation to the creation. He is not said to be the head of his body, the universe, nor is he merely Lord over the church.
   B. His resurrection life animates and nourishes and leads his church, as vine and branches (John 15:1ff).The purpose of all this is that "in all things [church as well as creation] he might have the pre-eminence."

J. B. Phillips had us pegged when he wrote his book *Your God Is Too Small*. The cosmic Christ is bigger, older, and stronger than anything or anyone in all creation. So-called "higher beings" are so much lower than he as to be of no consequence. Christ alone is worthy of our worship.

40

The Everliving Lord

Scripture Reading: Revelation 1:8

There is something intriguing about the concept of time. Physicists tell us there is a "space-time continuum" and that time is the fourth dimension. Human imagination has explored the possibility of time travel from H. G. Wells's *The Time Machine* to Steven Spielberg's *Back to the Future*.

Our finite minds can scarcely comprehend the yawning eons of geologic ages, much less the idea of eternity. And yet the aged apostle John, exiled on the Isle of Patmos, had a vision some nineteen hundred years ago of the Everliving Lord, who

I. Existed Before the Commencement of Time ("I am the Alpha . . . which was")

    A. Time has not always existed. There was a "time" before time began when nothing existed but God: no matter, no energy, nothing. Before creation, in the misty, mysterious antiquity of eternity past, there was only the Triune God.

    B. John had already shared this truth about the eternal nature of Christ in the opening words of his Gospel (John 1:1, 2).

II. Exists Throughout the Course of Time ("which is")

    A. When God appeared to Moses at the burning bush he identified himself as "the God of thy father, the God of Abraham . . . Isaac, and . . . Jacob" (Exod. 3:6). He is the God of every believer of every age.

    B. Jesus is truly "Christ our contemporary." He is the

Lord not only of the patriarchs and the prophets of the Old Testament but also of the disciples and apostles of the New. He is our Lord as well, for he is the God of history, existing equally in all times and in all places.

III. Will Exist After the Consummation of Time ("I am . . . the Omega . . . which is to come")
   A. Just as Christ existed before time began, he will continue to exist after it has ended. He is above and beyond and outside of time and is unaffected by it.
   B. "When the trumpet of the Lord shall sound and time shall be no more," Jesus Christ shall not cease to exist. Nor shall we, for we shall be in him and God shall be all in all (*see* 1 Cor. 15:24–28).

The Everliving Lord is timeless and eternal. "One day is with the Lord as a thousand years, and a thousand years as one day" (2 Peter 3:8). It is all the same to him.

We should not fret about his apparent delay in returning. He shall come again in his own good *time*.